THE WORLD'S GREATEST TENORS
CARRERAS DOMINGO PAVAROTTI

THE WORLD'S GREATEST TENORS
CARRERAS DOMINGO PAVAROTTI

MILLICENT JONES

JG PRESS

Published in the USA 1995 by
JG Press
Distributed by World
Publications, Inc.

The JG Press imprint is a
trademark of
JG Press, Inc.
455 Somerset Avenue
North Dighton, MA 02764

Produced by
Brompton Books
Corporation
15 Sherwood Place
Greenwich, Connecticut
06830

ISBN 1-57215-056-4

Printed in Spain

PAGE ONE: *Carreras,
Domingo, and Pavarotti
rehearsing the medley from
their first concert together in
Rome, 1990.*

PAGES 2-3: *Los Angeles hosts
the tenors' concert at Dodger
Stadium.*

THESE PAGES: *In their first
concert together, Carreras,
Domingo, and Pavarotti
perform at the Baths of
Caracalla in Rome.*

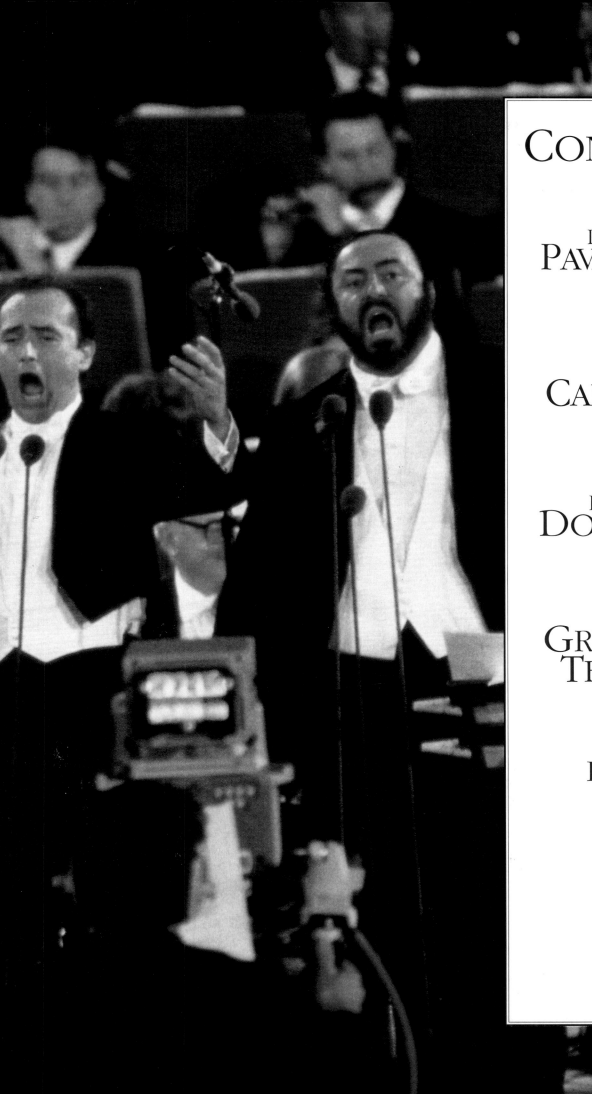

CONTENTS

LUCIANO
PAVAROTTI

RIGHT: *Flashing his famous smile, the tenor enjoys himself in some post-concert revelry.*

LEFT: *Pavarotti thanks an appreciative audience during the 1994 concert at Dodger Stadium.*

For many, Luciano Pavarotti ranks number one among the world's great tenors. His career has been marked by a dedication to the craft of singing combined with a heartfelt desire to communicate to the largest possible audience. He has never shied away from making himself accessible to the public, to the disdain of some opera cognoscenti. The success he enjoys among opera lovers and the general public alike testifies to his enormous talent as a singer as well as his irresistible charm.

Born on October 12th, 1935 in Modena, north-eastern Italy, Luciano exhibited an early love for music. His initial exposure to music came through his father, also a tenor, who often listened to opera at home. Pavarotti's earliest influences were the great Italian tenors Beniamino Gigli, Enrico Caruso,

ABOVE: *Celebrating the publication of* Pavarotti *written by Adua, his wife of over 30 years. Adua has always taken an active role in promoting and supporting her husband's career, as well as developing her own as an artistic manager.*

RIGHT: *Pavarotti plays Rodolfo in the 1978 production of* Luisa Miller *at London's Covent Garden opposite the beautiful soprano Katia Ricciarelli. Pavarotti views this as one of the more challenging roles in the Verdi repertoire due to its demands on both singing and acting abilities.*

and Giovanni Martinelli. But his early enthusiasm did not always meet with favor. An impromptu recital of "La Donna è Mobile" from Verdi's *Rigoletto* at the age of five annoyed the neighbors in his tenement block as they all yelled at him to keep quiet.

Undaunted by this early criticism, he joined a small church choir where his father also sang. However his voice was not his only concern at this early age. Like many Italian boys his age, his first love was for soccer. He played on the local team and would often spend six or seven hours a day practicing. He even considered becoming an athletics instructor after graduation from high school. Fortunately, after hearing a con-

cert rehearsal by Beniamino Gigli, one of the most famous tenors of his day, his mind was made up.

Gigli was performing in Modena and Luciano was allowed into the theater to hear him rehearse. Overwhelmed by his performance, Pavarotti approached him afterward and enthusiastically announced his desire to become a great tenor when he grew up. Gigli said that was a fine ambition. When Pavarotti asked how long Gigli had spent studying, he responded that he studied every day and that he would never stop studying. This made a great impression on the young boy; even the great Gigli, at the height of his powers, was still learning and studying.

Pavarotti began serious vocal studies in 1954 at the age of 19 in Modena and Mantua. His first teacher was Arrigo Pola, a professional tenor. The repetitiveness of the exercises required for vocal training did not bother the young tenor. He was fascinated by the different types of sound that the voice was able to produce. Pola soon discovered that Pavarotti possessed perfect pitch, an invaluable resource for any would-be singer.

Lessons with Pola did not take up all of Pavarotti's time. He took a part-time teaching job for two years during his studies, to supplement the financial help he received from his parents. He did not especially enjoy teaching young children; they found him rather a pushover and he had trouble controlling his classroom. However, his teaching position led to a more lucrative part-time job in insurance sales. After school he approached the parents of his pupils and persuaded them of the value of his life insurance. Although he was quite successful as a salesman, delivering sales pitches was hard on his burgeoning voice and eventually he had to give it up.

Nearly six years after his lessons with Pola began, and with increasing doubts about his fledgling career, Pavarotti entered his first vocal competition, the

ABOVE LEFT: *Dame Joan Sutherland, a long-time friend and colleague, accepts an award with Pavarotti at the 1991 Gramophone Awards.*

ABOVE: *In the 1982 movie,* Yes, Giorgio, *Pavarotti plays a tenor, Giorgio Fini, whose throat disorder can be cured only by the attentions of the lovely lady doctor shown in this photo.*

LEFT: Commedia del l'arte: *In true vaudevillian style, a pie-throwing food fight provides an amusing climax to the movie* Yes, Giorgio.

ABOVE: *On his tour of China, Pavarotti meets Mr. Liu Shirong, Deputy Director of the Central Opera Theater of China. Not a fan of Chinese cuisine, Pavarotti brought plenty of Italian food with him on this trip.*

RIGHT: *Pavarotti breaks ground for a new complex near his stables in Modena, Italy. This complex staged the Pavarotti International Horse Trials in September, 1991. The singer loves horses and goes riding whenever he can.*

Achille Peri competition held in Reggio Emilia in 1961. He won the competition and was given the chance to sing the role of Rodolfo in Puccini's *La Bohème* at the Teatro Municipale in Reggio Emilia. He was extremely excited about his debut, not only because it was his first real public appearance, but because Reggio Emilians were traditional rivals to his home town of Modena, adding additional incentive to prove himself. The critics reviewed his performance favorably. "The tenor Luciano Pavarotti sang with estimable good taste and with vivid musicality, likewise displaying vocal equipment both penetrating and flexible. He was liked perhaps more than his colleagues," said the *Nova Gazetta di Reggio Emilia*. Among the

audience was Alessandro Ziliani, an influential agent from Milan, who was to guide Pavarotti in his early career.

This was an exciting time for Pavarotti both professionally and personally. Pavarotti met and married his wife, Adua, in late 1961 and his first daughter, Lorenza, was born just a year later. Adua was a Modena native like himself and she worked as a primary school teacher during the early years of their marriage. As his fame increased, she proved a shrewd businesswoman in managing the financial concerns of the Pavarotti family and now acts as the official Pavarotti archivist as well.

After his debut, he made his next appearance at Lucca in another production of *La Bohème*. This performance

did not go as well as his first, partly due to the fact that the female lead in the production, a singer past her prime, believed she was being upstaged by the young man. Nonetheless, Pavarotti weathered the diva's temper and went on to sing the same role in Dublin. It was in Dublin that he was "discovered" by the non-Italian musical world. Joan Ingpen, an artistic administrator then working at Covent Garden, was eager to recruit a lesser known artist to serve as backup for an upcoming production of *La Bohème*. After seeing his Rodolfo, Ingpen approached him to cover for Giuseppe di Stefano who was to perform the role at Covent Garden.

Di Stefano, at that time rather advanced in his career, sang in only one performance of the production, leaving Pavarotti an ample showcase for his talents. His performance attracted the attention of the administrators of Glyndebourne Opera who recruited him for the role of Idamante in Mozart's *Idomeneo* in the 1962 season. Pavarotti was not used to the strict performance practice which Glyndebourne maintained and his sometimes extravagant Italian musical gestures did not fit in with the Glyndebourne style. He appreciated the chance to polish his vocal technique, however, and his associates remarked on his eagerness to learn and intellectual capabilities. Sir George Christie, who runs the opera from his family

LEFT: *Pavarotti's debut as Manrico in a 1975 performance of* Il Trovatore *at the San Francisco Opera. Joan Sutherland proclaimed his rendition of "Di quella pira" "unforgettable."*

ABOVE: *Pavarotti and the Princess: after torrential rain had accompanied the singer's recital in London's Hyde Park, Pavarotti brightens his evening as he kisses the hand of Princess Diana. The Prince and Princess later joined him for dinner at the Hyde Park Hotel.*

estate in East Sussex, referred to him as "one of nature's virtues."

Pavarotti's career really took off when he embarked on a tour of Australia with Joan Sutherland and Richard Bonynge in 1965. He became friends with the couple when he appeared at Covent Garden for the first time. Sutherland took a special interest in him because he was unusually tall for a tenor, which complemented her stature on stage. The tour was exhausting for all involved, with performances of *La Sonnambula, L'Elisir d'Amore, Lucia di Lammermoor,* and *La Traviata* in four cities. Sutherland and Pavarotti were well suited to one another both physically and artistically. As Sutherland later said: "He can take a stand on doing something his way – but you can always work it out with Luciano."

Soon after the tour ended, and with his international career firmly established, Pavarotti made his debut at La Scala, Milan, as the Duke of Mantua in Verdi's *Rigoletto.* Pavarotti believes that his debut at the most prominent of Italian opera houses was delayed by the fact that Italians do not promote their own singers until they achieve recognition abroad first. La Scala was duly impressed by him, however, and he was invited back to create the role of Tebaldo in Bellini's *I Capuleti e i Montecchi.*

In the same year, Pavarotti made his American debut in Miami, again teaming up with Joan Sutherland in a per-

formance of *Lucia.* The Miami Opera Association needed a replacement for tenor Renalto Cioni a few weeks before the performance and Sutherland suggested the young tenor. His performance achieved critical acclaim, although the director, Anthony Stivanello, worked hard with Pavarotti to improve his acting in the role of Edgardo.

Acting has always been a challenge for Pavarotti. A critic once said: "Mr. Pavarotti never went out of character. Then how could he? He never got in it." His appearance in the movie *Yes, Giorgio* in 1982, where he plays a famous Italian tenor who falls in love with his

BELOW: *A true indication of his status as a cultural icon, Pavarotti poses beside his waxwork at Madame Tussaud's.*

RIGHT: *Chefs look on as Pavarotti enjoys his cake at a recent birthday celebration.*

LEFT: *Pavarotti as the peasant Nemorino (literally "little nobody") in the Royal Opera House's 1991 production of* L'Elisir d'Amore.

RIGHT: *Pavarotti clowns around with Joanne Woodward and Paul Newman after a performance of Leoncavallo's* Pagliacci.

throat doctor on tour in America, did not do much to belie this opinion. His warmth and charm as a person come through in the film, but there is a sense that he is not acting, merely playing himself. This tendency is not unknown among great opera stars, which might have something to do with why they are so venerated both on and off stage. Their admirers feel that they *are* the great romantic, powerful, villainous, or seductive characters they play on stage. Pavarotti himself admits that he feels most comfortable in the romantic roles of the Italian opera repertoire, as they most closely resemble his own attitudes and feelings toward life.

It was in one of the great roles of Italian opera, Rodolfo in *La Bohème*, that Pavarotti made his debut at the Metropolitan Opera House in New York. A debut at the Met is one of the crucial tests of any singer, and Pavarotti was suitably excited and fearful of the prospect. Having come from wonderfully-received performances at the San Francisco Opera, the New York audience was eager to hear him.

Unfortunately, Pavarotti came down with a bad case of the flu just a week prior to his first performance. He post-

poned his appearance for a week in the hope that he would recover. On the day of the performance, he tried out his voice with one of the administrators of the Met, who thought that he sounded well enough to perform. With the unflagging assistance of Mirella Freni, his Modenese co-star and close friend, he managed to get through the performance.

The critics and public did not take much notice of his illness. A New York critic commented: "Any tenor who can toss off high Cs with such abandon, successfully negotiate delicate diminuendo effects and attack Puccinian phrases so fervently is going to win over any *La Bohème* audience and Mr. Pavarotti had them eating out of his hand." Pavarotti was unable to make it through the second performance, however, and was forced to return to Modena where he spent three months recuperating. The whole experience was terribly disappointing, but he returned to the Met in 1972 with Joan Sutherland in a performance of *L'Elisir d'Amore*. In an effortless display of virtuosity Pavarotti sang the nine high Cs required by his part and the New York audiences quickly forgot about the aborted 1968 debut.

His appearance at the Met caused his career to quickly mushroom. Around this time he became associated with Herbert Breslin, who initially looked after his publicity and then later became his manager. After a trial run of recitals in the Midwest, Breslin encouraged him to do his first solo recital at Carnegie Hall in 1973, which was an instant sellout. As his fame increased, stadium concerts with tickets priced at $100 each and more became the norm.

He has done his share of free public concerts, however. His remarkable "Pavarotti in the Park" concert in June 1993 attracted an audience of 500,000, and was broadcast on television to millions more. In July 1991, he performed to an audience of over 150,000 in London's Hyde Park. The performance was as memorable for the torrential rain that poured all evening as well as for the performance given.

In addition to his live performances, Pavarotti's impact on the classical recording world has been profound. His recordings have continued to outsell those of any other classical artist, and he was the first ever classical artist to reach the number one position in the UK pop album charts with his "Essential Pavarotti." "Essential Pavarotti II" duplicated this success by reaching number one in 1991. His famous rendition of "Nessun Dorma" from Puccini's *Turandot* became the signature tune for the 1990 World Cup.

Despite his frenetic schedule, Pavarotti has always set time aside to pursue a life outside the musical world. His beloved villa at Pesaro, on the east coast of Italy, is a welcome retreat from the stage. In the beautiful house overlooking the Adriatic, he can indulge in his favorite pastimes: horsemanship, painting, and, of course, eating.

He first became interested in horses on a visit to Ireland. After persuading his three daughters to take lessons there, he purchased some horses and set up a stable on his Italian estate. His horse, Shaughran, is a huge 18 hands, and seems able to accommodate his weight without noticing. In September 1991, Pavarotti launched the International Horse Trials at Modena. This competition is held on an annual basis and brings together show jumpers from all over the world. It is unique in the world of horse trials in that it has a distinctly musical aspect, with performances by the Salzburg Festival Orchestra and various choirs. Pavarotti enjoys watching and socializing with people who enjoy horses as much as he does.

Painting also has its attractions for the singer. Playing Cavaradossi in a production of *Tosca*, he was encouraged to use real oil paints on stage to bring the character to life as much as possible. He found painting off stage to be a relaxing hobby which allows him to focus on creating art, rather than merely reproducing it. His paintings, with their bright colors and simple themes, were good enough to attract the attention of a Milanese gallery, which now organizes exhibitions of his work.

Eating has always been a big part of Pavarotti's life. He enjoys cooking as much as eating and is never far from a supply of Italian food. On tour in China in 1986, he made it part of his contract to have a supply of Italian ingredients with him wherever he went. He ended up hiring a famous Italian restauranteur and chef to travel with him, along with

crates of olive oil, pasta, Parmesan and the like. He was never far from the famous spaghetti which he loves so much.

Pavarotti's size is something that he has fought and continues to struggle against. When he is dieting, he has a special dinner of cold vegetables and chicken which he swears by. He claims to know the number of calories in every item of food, and is always concerned with his blood pressure and his general physical state. Despite his best efforts, Pavarotti simply loves his food, and finds it difficult to live in moderation. His size has definitely affected his career, forcing him to record some roles rather than perform them live, if,

for example, the character requires a lot of movement on stage. As his career started to peak, he went through a bout of deep depression over his weight, which only a close brush with death was able to cure.

In 1975, returning from New York to Milan, the plane on which he was flying had to make a crash landing due to fog. When the plane hit the ground, it broke into two and people struggled to get out. Stranded out at the end of the runway and having lost contact with the control tower, it was a couple of hours before vehicles arrived to take the passengers back to the terminal. The weather was very chilly and damp, and Pavarotti quickly seconded a large

FAR LEFT: *Pavarotti playfully embraces a china replica of himself. The merchandising of Pavarotti has been extremely successful, and he has appeared in a variety of advertisements, including one for Blackglama furs.*

ABOVE: *Pavarotti kisses the hand of the Queen Mum. A peasant by birth, Pavarotti has scaled the heights and royalty are not immune to the powers of his voice.*

LEFT: *Pavarotti has a variety of talismans that he carries on stage to ensure good luck for his performances. One of these is a bent nail, which he must find just before going on stage. As everyone backstage is now aware of this ritual, a nail is planted for him before his arrival.*

ABOVE: *Sting and Pavarotti pose for the camera. Despite their differences of style, the two men have both spent time at the top of the pop charts.*

RIGHT: *Pavarotti's huge white handkerchief has become something of a trademark and he refuses to perform without it. He has even been known to take refuge underneath it at difficult recitals.*

handkerchief from a friendly passenger to wrap around his throat. He was obviously very shaken by this experience and says it made him re-evaluate his life. "The shock of having come that close to death cured me completely of my disinterest in life. The cure was so thorough, I immediately set to work and study with the kind of energy and enthusiasm I had when I started vocal studies at 19." He also immediately embarked upon a diet for the first time, during which he lost 80 pounds.

In the last few years, Pavarotti has added new operas to his repertoire, including the challenging *Pagliacci* by Leoncavallo and *Otello* by Guiseppe Verdi. He performed the latter opera in a concert version accompanied by Kiri Te Kanawa and Leo Nucci under the direction of Georg Solti with the Chicago Symphony Orchestra. The role is a very difficult one, and he was not too

proud to sit in on some of Placido Domingo's rehearsals of the role, as he prepared for his performance at the Metropolitan Opera. The preparation paid off: "His voice sounded the music with a thrilling clarity and firmness of word and tone . . . in Otello's blazing monologues he was brilliant," said one critic of his performance.

Pavarotti continues to enjoy a tremendous rapport with his public which will undoubtedly endure. He is especially interested, at this point in his career, in developing the future of opera and opera singers, along with his wife Adua, who runs an artists management company. Each year in Modena he holds an international vocal competition for young singers. These singers then join him in a series of concerts at world-famous concert halls, where his presence can only encourage them to become the Pavarottis of tomorrow.

JOSE
CARRERAS

LEFT: *Carreras, in fine voice, delights the audience at Dodger Stadium, Los Angeles, 1994.*

RIGHT: *Carreras shows no signs of the devastating leukemia which he endured in 1987-88 as he smiles for the camera. Many were worried that the chemotherapy he underwent would affect his vocal cords, but their fears were allayed when he returned to perform in splendid voice in 1988.*

ABOVE: *Carreras in the role of Alfredo in Verdi's* La Traviata *opposite Romanian soprano Ileana Cotrubas at London's Covent Garden. Alfredo confesses his love for Violetta in the famous duet "Un dì felice" ("Happy one day").*

RIGHT: *Carreras gives it his all in a rehearsal for the historical 1994 concert in Los Angeles' Dodger Stadium.*

José Carreras is known not only for his terrific talent as a singer but also for his ability to fight and overcome personal adversity. His career has led him to all the great opera houses of Europe and America, where he has been universally admired, and a triumphant return to the stage in 1988 after a fierce battle with leukemia was welcomed with immense appreciation by both his fans and colleagues alike.

Carreras was born in the Catalonian region of Spain on December 5th, 1946. The conditions in Spain at this time were very poor as the Spanish Civil War had left the country in economic ruin. Carreras' father Josep Carreras-Soler had fought in the war as a Republican and found it difficult to resume his job as a school teacher under the Franco regime. The family therefore decided,

ABOVE: *Singing "Una furtiva lagrima," one of the most popular of all tenor arias from Donizetti's humorous* L'Elisir d'Amore. *This lovely melody is sung by Nemorino as he sees his love, Adina, weep with regret.*

RIGHT: *Carreras has sometimes wondered whether the touring life of the modern opera singer suited him. He says however, that when he does have a moment to himself, he doesn't know what to do. His priorities have shifted slightly, however, since his illness, and he seems to want a more balanced life.*

FAR RIGHT: *In December 1988, soon after recovering from the leukemia that nearly killed him, Carreras makes an appearance at the French fashion house, Celine. Celine sponsored him in a gala banquet in Paris to raise money for his leukemia research foundation.*

like many others at the time, to seek opportunity abroad. The Carreras family journeyed to Argentina but soon became homesick for Spain and unhappy with the dire conditions of South America. They decided to return to their home country after 11 months and moved to a working-class suburb of Barcelona. As Josep was still unable to get a position, his mother, Antonia Coll-Saigi, opened up a hairdressing salon in their home which proved an excellent source of income and provided Carreras with his first stage.

Carreras was blessed with a happy childhood and enjoyed playing soccer and handball at school. He even made the school's championship basketball team despite his height. Surprisingly, his family was not especially interested in music and his first experience with opera actually happened through the cinema. On one of his usual weekend visits to the movies he saw *The Great Caruso* starring Mario Lanza. This film, much like the rehearsal by Beniamino Gigli that Pavarotti attended, caused a sort of musical epiphany to occur in the

young boy. As he says in his autobiography, *Singing from the Soul*, the movie "stirred up a desire I didn't know I had. It made me want to sing." From then on, he began to sing arias from the movie constantly, even though he had never heard them before. His parents were delighted to discover this hidden talent, although the unceasing vocalization caused their nerves to become a bit frayed. Carreras was sometimes forced to retreat to the bathroom in order to sing his favorite aria, "La Donna è Mobile."

Although his parents were not interested in opera, they decided to buy a record player and the soundtrack from *The Great Caruso*. The young José was thrilled at the chance to sing along with his hero. He even began giving impromptu recitals in his mother's salon. The tips he received from the appreciative clientele were enough to buy candy and small toys.

At the age of eight, Carreras went to Barcelona's Teatro del Liceo with his father to see Verdi's *Aida* starring the famous soprano Renata Tebaldi. This performance created a deep impression on him: "It was the first time in my life that I'd stepped into a theater, but the place was as familiar to me as if I had always known it . . . from the moment I crossed the threshold, I knew it was my world . . ." His parents began taking his musical interests more seriously and when an opportunity to appear on the radio came, they encouraged him to do it.

The broadcast, made at Christmas time for the National Radio of Spain, was a benefit concert for needy children. Carreras sang alongside famous tenors of the day, including Mario del Monaco, who was then appearing at the Teatro del Liceo. His performance included a Catalan Christmas carol and his beloved "La Donna è Mobile." The broadcast was very successful and prompted his first live appearance on the operatic stage.

The management of the Liceo theater called him a few months later to ask if he would be willing to perform the role of a small boy in an opera by Manuel de Falla, *El Retablo de Maese Pedro*. The

ABOVE: *Carreras traveled with conductor Zubin Mehta to Sarajevo in June, 1994 to perform with the Sarajevo Philharmonic Orchestra in the country's national library, destroyed by the war which has ravaged the city.*

RIGHT: *José Carreras poses with a bevy of beautiful showbusiness personalities.*

Liceo at that time was the most prestigious opera house in Spain and the performance was to be conducted by the famous Spanish pianist, Jose Iturbi. The family agreed that José should perform, and after three months preparing for the first rehearsal with his first music teacher Magda Prunera, he sang his solo for the great Iturbi. Iturbi was deeply moved by the young boy's voice, and his performance in the opera was a great success. Carreras sang in two more small roles at the Liceo before his voice broke in 1959.

Carreras' formal training as a singer began in 1964 at the age of 18 with Francisco Puig, but was interrupted by his mother's sudden death from cancer the following year. Her death affected him greatly and in later years her last words to him, "I know that you will be someone very important," were to haunt him. He felt that he needed to be more careful and practical with his life

after her death and therefore engaged in a chemistry course at the University of Barcelona in order to help out in the family's cosmetics business.

After three years of study with Puig, Carreras became dissatisfied and engaged Juan Ruax as a teacher. Ruax, a dental technician by trade, had never sung professionally, although he had a wonderful tenor voice. Ruax helped Carreras through lengthy discussions about the role of interpretation over technique. They would listen to records of the great tenors together and talk about their particular style and virtues. Little time was spent actually singing in these lessons; indeed Carreras maintains that Ruax taught him ways *not* to sing which were to prove extremely valuable.

As his studies drew to a close in 1968, Carreras faced a difficult decision. Should he continue with his studies in chemistry or devote his life to a career in singing? Luckily for the world of opera, he decided that singing was his true love and that he would pursue it as a career. The decision began to pay off after a friend suggested that he sing for Fernandez Cid, a famous Spanish music critic, in order to appear on his television show. The critic was duly impressed and invited him to perform.

The wide exposure he received through the show was a stepping stone to his audition with the Gran Teatro del Liceo, where he had sung as a boy. His first adult role was Flavio in Bellini's *Norma*, which premiered in January 1970. Critics praised his performance and predicted a successful future for him on stage. It was during this time that he became good friends with Montserrat Caballé, whose brother Carlos now acts as his artistic manager. At her request, and to the envy of more experienced singers in the company, he performed the role of Gennaro in Donizetti's *Lucrezia Borgia.*

Carreras' big break came in July 1971 when he won the prestigious Verdi Singing Competition in Parma, Italy, singing a *romanza* from *Un Ballo in Maschera*. The contest has traditionally been viewed as a springboard to the big time, and he made the most of his success there. As a result, he landed the role of Rodolfo in *La Bohème* at the Parma Opera. One of the most important contacts he made there was with Guiseppe di Stefano, the foremost Italian tenor of his day. Stefano was also instrumental in inspiring the young Pavarotti.

Later in 1971, Carreras' tour of the major opera houses in Europe began, with performances in Barcelona, Madrid, and Minorca. The operas he played in were astonishingly wide-ranging for a tenor at the start of his career and included *Maria Stuarda, I Lombardi, Lucia di Lammermoor, Rigoletto,* and *Luisa Miller*. He then progressed to the United States where his appearance in Puccini's *Madama Butterfly* at the newly formed New York City Opera at Lincoln Center guaranteed him a place in the hearts and minds of Americans. It was in New York that his style and stage persona became crystalized and that he came to discover his

distinct interpretive style. A fondly-recalled moment from that period was when the great (both artistically and physically) Birgit Nilsson embraced him as "my baby Cavaradossi."

A moment that Carreras certainly would sooner forget occurred at his next great debut at the Vienna Staatsoper in January, 1974. At the end of one of his most favorite arias, "La Donna è Mobile," his voice suddenly gave out and he could not continue; the last

notes simply would not come out. Although the Vienna audiences surely noticed that something was amiss, they still applauded politely and continue to welcome him back.

Carreras' La Scala debut in 1975 was an important event which looked forward to the future of opera while retaining a romantic link with the past. He appeared as Riccardo in *Un Ballo in Maschera*, one of his favorite roles. Di Stefano, the tenor who he had met years before and who had become a good friend, was present at one of the rehearsals and noticed that Carreras' costume did not fit him properly. He immediately took him back to the vast costume collection in his apartment and offered him the costume that he had worn at La Scala many years previously in the very same role. The La Scala audiences became aware of this event, and his debut was welcomed as an extraordinary occasion.

One of Carreras' favorite conductors was the late Herbert von Karajan. Although some performers were put off by his perceived coolness and unapproachability, Carreras found him a very supportive and caring artist. Carreras was recommended to him for a role in a 1976 production of the Verdi *Requiem* by one of his associates who had seen his La Scala performance. Karajan asked him to come to a rehearsal of the piece scheduled for 11 am, a time of day when most singers are still asleep. He was extremely nervous about the rehearsal, and got up at 5 am to make sure that his voice was ready by the appointed time. Alas, to his great consternation, his voice would not cooperate and gave out almost immediately. He thought that his chance to impress the stern von Karajan had disappeared completely. Von Karajan offered encouragement, however, and soon after asked him to appear in Verdi's *Don Carlos* at Salzburg.

Throughout the late 1970s and 1980s, Carreras was a frequent performer on the international opera circuit. Performances at Salzburg, the Metropolitan Opera, and Vienna as well as numerous recording contracts and films kept him extremely busy. In an effort to bring more listeners to opera through popular music, he recorded Leonard Bernstein's *West Side Story* with Kiri Te Kanawa, Tatiana Troyanos, and the composer himself conducting. He also starred in *Final Romance*, a film based on the life of tenor Julián Gayarre.

His hectic and challenging artistic schedule, planned years in advance, came to an abrupt halt in July 1987. He was to begin filming *La Bohème* in Paris when a painful toothache started to

bother him. He had been feeling exhausted and depressed for a few weeks, but he blamed it on his busy schedule. The toothache became so bad he was unable to sing and went to the American Hospital in Paris for treatment. The toothache was merely a symptom of a much greater problem. The doctors kept him in the hospital for a few days, did some tests, and eventually diagnosed leukemia. The diagnosis was especially devastating as his mother had also died of cancer and he knew the immense challenge that was to face him if he wanted to survive. His blood platelet level was dangerously low and he flew to Barcelona almost immediately to undergo chemotherapy.

The chemotherapy was extremely painful, but his love of opera saw him through. He sang arias in his head while being treated so he could determine exactly how long he had before the treatment was done. The chemotherapy was not effective enough on its own to cure the disease so he had to fly to

ABOVE: *Carreras sings in* La Traviata. *He says a recording of this opera would be a definite choice for his imaginary desert island, along with Mozart's* The Marriage of Figaro *and Rossini's* The Barber of Seville.

RIGHT: *The singer admires Ileana Cotrubas in* L'Elisir d'Amore. *Cotrubas has been lauded for both her outstanding vocal technique as well as her expressive and emotive acting.*

ABOVE: *Conductor Zubin Mehta embraces Carreras after the tenors' encore at Dodger Stadium in Los Angeles. Mehta and Carreras recently teamed up again for a premiere of Verdi's* Jerusalem *at the Vienna State Opera.*

RIGHT: *Carreras singing solo at the July 16th, 1994 concert. Carreras was the motivating force which brought the three men together in 1990, and he was glad to reunite with them in another legendary performance.*

FAR RIGHT, ABOVE: *Montserrat Caballé and Carreras joining together for a concert to launch Spain's Cultural Olympiad in 1988.*

Seattle, Washington to undergo a bone marrow transplant. The transplant was successful, eventually, but not until he was treated with an experimental drug to help the new bone marrow "take."

His near brush with death gave Carreras a new appreciation of his life and family. While in hospital he received thousands of letters from fans (one addressed "Tenor, Seattle"), royalty, and colleagues. He was given great encouragement and support by his so-called "rivals" Pavarotti and Domingo. Pavarotti sent him a telegram saying "José get well. Otherwise I won't have any competition." Domingo, who had had his differences with him in the past, telephoned him often, and took time out to visit him in Seattle.

He returned to Spain in February, 1987 and spent nearly a year recuperat-ing from his illness. He was very wor-ried about the condition of his voice, because leukemia treatments can some-times affect the vocal chords. He was re-lieved to discover that his voice seemed in fine working order, however, and he gradually began using it a small amount each day. He also used this time to establish the José Carreras International Leukemia Foundation in Barcelona.

July 21st, 1988 saw his return to the concert stage. Thousands of Spaniards welcomed him back under the grand backdrop of Barcelona's Arch of Triumph where he sang a benefit con-cert for his Foundation. The event attracted over 30,000 including Queen Sofia of Spain, who had followed his pro-gress and sent telegrams to him in Seattle. He describes this concert as the beginning of his own personal, physical,

spiritual, and artistic renaissance.

He gave another memorable concert later that year at the Vienna Staatsoper. As the crowd cheered him as he came on the stage, and displayed a huge "Will-kommen José" banner from the bal-cony, he found it difficult to control his emotions: "The effervescent mood in the house expanded and enveloped the stage." The concert lasted over three hours, and was transmitted live by Austrian television and to hundreds standing outside the opera house who had not been lucky enough to get seats.

Carreras has the ability to generate an emotional empathy among his listeners that is the envy of many singers. His courageous battle with death and his unwillingness to let it end his career will continue to inspire millions who see him as a hero, both on stage and off.

PLACIDO
DOMINGO

LEFT: *Domingo in his element at the tenors' concert in Dodger Stadium, Los Angeles, 1994.*

RIGHT: *Domingo in a recital appearance. The tenor does not sing as many recitals as Pavarotti and Carreras, preferring to devote his energies to operatic productions and conducting.*

BELOW: *Domingo enjoying a joke at a press conference in Madrid. However, after canceling a concert at Wembley Arena in London, he provoked headlines such as "The Tantrum of the Opera" and "Pique Performance."*

RIGHT: *The singing maestro rehearsing an audience at St. James Church in Prague for a special Christmas concert in 1990.*

Placido Domingo has been described as the "thinking man's tenor." His success has come from his rich velvety tenor voice and dark good looks combined with the ability to vividly portray whatever part he chooses. His artistic range has widened considerably in the last 10 years to encompass the Wagnerian repertoire as well as the Italian and he now includes conducting among his many artistic endeavors. Like both Carerras and Pavarotti, he too has suffered adversity and misunderstanding along the way. The Mexican earthquake of 1985 was a personal and professional milestone for him and many say he emerged from the disaster a more reflective and profound artist.

Domingo was born in Madrid on January 21st, 1941. His parents, Placido Domingo and Pepta Embil, were singers in the *zarzuela*, a popular form of Spanish operetta. Their company traveled to Latin America on tour in 1946, when Placido was five. They decided to stay in Mexico and were reunited with Placido in 1949. Placido, a born performer according to his mother, began to sing and play the piano in the company from the age of eight. He was interested in all types of music, but like many boys his age, soccer and girls were his top priority. He even played goalkeeper on his school team, which included three students who were to become professional soccer players.

He entered the National Conservatory of Music in his teens as a pianist. He does not remember a single overriding influence on his musical education there, but he gained a basic grounding in both vocal and instrumental music. Like many an operatic character, however, he fell in love with a woman at the tender age of 16 and secretly married her. She soon became pregnant, and Domingo had to forgo the life of a student to help support his new family. During this time, he worked in television as a sound effects technician, sang in over 180 performances of *My Fair Lady*, played the piano in a hotel lounge, and even tried his hand at acting. Not many tenors can count Chekhov's *Cherry Orchard* among their dramatic repertoire.

Two years after it had begun, this early marriage ended in divorce. After his enormously varied musical efforts to support himself, he decided to go for the big time and auditioned for the Mexican National Opera at the age of 18. He was offered a number of small roles and his career as an opera singer began. In one of his first tours of America, he sang the role of Edgardo in *Lucia di Lammermoor* opposite Lily Pons, in her

RIGHT: *Following in the footsteps of all the world's great tenors, Domingo plays Radamès in Verdi's classic* Aida. *The singer has recorded this opera three times.*

FAR RIGHT: *Grace Bumbry stars with Domingo in Meyerbeer's* L'Africaine. *In this opera, Domingo plays Vasco da Gama, the Portuguese explorer, who falls in love with Selika, the African queen of the title. After da Gama tires of her, Selika kills herself by breathing the scent of a poisonous tree.*

last Lucia. Pons had first sung the role in 1931 opposite the great Beniamino Gigli. In the same way as the great Di Stefano gave Carerras the *Un Ballo in Maschera* costume he had once worn, there was a great sense of operatic continuity in this performance, of the older generation of "greats" making way to welcome the new.

During his tenure with Mexican National Opera he met his wife-to-be, Marta Ornelas. They were married in 1962, and quickly departed to Tel Aviv for a six-month contract with the Hebrew National Opera. The Domingos ended up staying for nearly three years, and Domingo maintains it was a great learning experience for both him and his wife. The steady flow of nearly 200 performances in the hot climate during these years helped to increase his endurance as a singer.

In 1965 Marta became pregnant with their first child, Placi, and the couple left Israel. Marta eventually gave up her stage career after the birth of the couple's second child, but continues to be actively involved in managing Domingo's schedule of appearances. She is a pillar of support in an otherwise frenzied performing schedule.

In 1966 Domingo successfully debuted at the New York City Opera in a performance of Ginastera's *Don Rodrigo*. He was chosen for the opera by director Julius Rudel who, upon

ABOVE: *A huge fan of the composer Andrew Lloyd Webber, Domingo took part in a performance of the composer's "Requiem" with Sarah Brightman, and Paul Miles-Kingston under the direction of conductor Lorin Maazel at Westminster Abbey, 1985.*

RIGHT: *Starring as a dapper Andrea Chenier in the opera of the same name in a 1985 Covent Garden performance. Domingo's voice has been described as "magnificent, warm and sensual, smooth and caressing in quality, possessing a beautiful falsettone, penetrating high notes, and a clear but passionate declamation."*

initial impression, thought the singer would be a great star "if he sung half as well as he looked." Ginastera himself was in the audience on opening night and was reportedly moved to tears by Domingo's performance. The performance celebrated the opening of the company's glamorous new residence at Lincoln Center and was a great success, marking the beginning of New York's affair with the singer.

His Met debut was in 1968 as Maurizio in *Adriana Lecouvreur*. A few days before his scheduled performance, he received a phone call late in the afternoon from Rudolf Bing, general manager of the Metropolitan, asking him if he would replace Franco Corelli that night in the production of *Lecouvreur*. He had spent all day in stage rehearsals for *Turandot*, and had not had any time to warm up his voice. Bing's

persistence won out, however, and Domingo warmed up in his cab on the way to Lincoln Center, to the great surprise of passing motorists.

The Met has been a frequent home for Domingo, and he has performed there over 400 times in 34 different roles. He has, of course, been a favorite all over the world, with performances at La Scala, Covent Garden, and the Vienna Staatsoper, to name but a few. In 1983 he made his conducting debut with *Die Fledermaus* at Covent Garden. Many artists have tried to make the leap from performer to conductor without success. Domingo, however, has made this aspect of his career a priority, and has built up an impressive repertoire, including *Macbeth*, *La Traviata*, *Rigoletto*, *Barber of Seville*, and *La Bohème* among others. He is popular among both singers and audiences in these

efforts and is known to be sympathetic toward his performers. Having experienced life on the stage he will modulate his conducting to accommodate a tricky vocal passage or long phrase. One performer commented: "I think what gives Placido the real edge is how much he understands the psychological game of playing opera. It's a bit like the psychological game of playing tennis — you know, when to push, when to draw back, when to be sympathetic. He just knows instinctively how to get the best out of us."

Domingo has also been quite active in performing popular music, perhaps the best known example of which is his recording with John Denver entitled "Perhaps Love." Although these efforts have been criticized he maintains that he loves singing "anything that is good music." The money he makes through

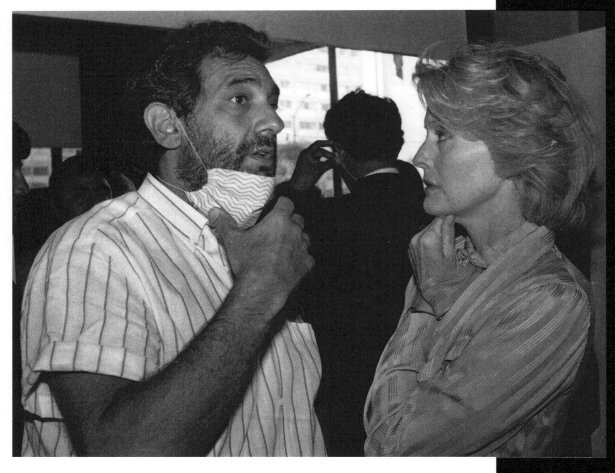

ABOVE: *On September 19th, 1985 a devastating earthquake hit Mexico. Domingo returned there immediately to aid in the rescue efforts and to search for four missing relatives. Domingo took a year off from his performing schedule to perform benefit concerts for earthquake victims. In this photo, he talks with the wife of the U.S. Ambassador to Mexico, Constance Gavin, at the Tlatelolco Family Service Center, Mexico City.*

RIGHT: *Composer Gian Carlo Menotti embraces Domingo backstage following the world premiere of Menotti's* Goya, *a portrait of the Spanish painter. This opera was composed specifically for Domingo and was premiered in November, 1986 at the John F. Kennedy Center for the Performing Arts.*

these recordings is also a consideration. "When I record an opera," he says, "the effort is enormous but the sales low. *Oberon* or *Aida* won't provide much of an income for my children or grand-children, but they may stand to benefit from an album like 'Perhaps Love.'" He also thinks it is important to expose more people to opera by getting them interested in his voice, which then might bring them to the opera house. He doesn't rule out performing any type of music, and is especially attracted to the works of Andrew Lloyd Webber, whose memorable tunes have been enjoyed by millions. Certainly other tenors, both contemporary and historical, have enjoyed popularity among a mass audience so why should Domingo be an exception?

During the mid-1980s, Domingo's schedule was horrendously busy. He had given over 2500 performances, sung nearly 100 different roles and recorded more than any tenor in the history of the opera world. The Mexican earthquake of 1985 changed his attitude toward work, however. "I was touched

by tragedy, by loss and I think as a result my priorities shifted." He lost several extended family members in the quake and was actually involved in the rescue effort, some say to the detriment of his voice which might have been affected by the dust. In addition, he set up an emergency village for 200 families and houses for those children orphaned by the quake. He took a year out of his schedule to sing benefit concerts which raised nearly $1.5 million for relief efforts.

After the earthquake, he began to become involved in a number of artistic projects with a Spanish or Latin focus. He agreed to become Artistic Consultant to the newly forming Los Angeles Opera, which represented the huge Hispanic presence in southern California, as well as Artistic Advisor to the Maestranza Opera in Seville. He starred in a new opera by Gian Carlo Menotti about the famous Spanish artist Goya, and in 1988 he performed with other Spanish and Latin American artists including Rosario Andrade, Gloria Estefan, and Linda Ronstadt in a concert on the lawn of Central Park.

The period after the earthquake was also marked by several highly publicized cancellations. In December 1986 he canceled a concert at Wembley, outside of London, less than 24 hours prior to its start because he thought the ticket prices (from around $30–$100) were too high. He announced the cancellation on a television chat show, but many audience members turned out only to be disappointed by his absence. The promoter, Jeffrey Kruger, was also somewhat disappointed, announcing that he wanted "the head of Placido Domingo." This rather rash act hurt his professional reputation. Suspicion about his true motives in canceling arose when it was found that at the time of his television announcement, only 2936 out of 9631 tickets had been sold. Skeptics thought that he might have felt this number too few to justify his presence on stage. After being sued by the promoter, he eventually settled out of court and agreed to do a benefit concert for Save The Children Fund in 1987 as a replacement for his original performance.

He seems to have emerged from this troubled time a more introspective and adventurous artist, stretching himself in the most difficult Wagnerian operas, including *Meistersinger, Parsifal, Die Walküre,* and *Tannhäuser*. Many tenors, having become successful in Italian opera are pleased to sing it forever. Domingo is always looking for a

FAR LEFT, BELOW: *Domingo poses with Queen Sofia of Spain and Gian Carlo Menotti. Although Domingo grew up in Mexico, he has recently strengthened his ties with Spain, his birthplace, serving as the Music Director for the 1992 Seville World's Fair.*

LEFT: *Domingo plays the Moor in Verdi's* Otello, *one of the most challenging tenor roles in the operatic repertoire. Sir Laurence Olivier commented that Domingo "acts the role of Othello as well as I do – and can sing it as well!"*

BELOW: *Domingo's versatility is seemingly unbounded. This photo shows a rehearsal with Gloria Estefan for a concert in New York's Central Park in 1988.*

new challenge, however, and his performances have gained the accolade of the most demanding audiences. He won his seventh Grammy Award for his recording of *Lohengrin* with Georg Solti. He did have some difficulties conforming to the niceties of German pronunciation, however. In a production of *Die Walküre* in Vienna, Domingo was coached by Christoph von Dohnányi in an effort to remove his Italianate singing style and produce the rough stresses and emphasis required by the German.

From his most recent activity, it is easy to see that he is preparing himself for the day when he will no longer perform on the operatic stage. He has agreed to become Artistic Director of the Washington Opera in 1996, and is president of the European Community Youth Opera. He also served as Music Director for the 1992 Seville World's Fair strengthening his tie with Spain, his birthplace. In an effort to give younger singers the chance to enter the profession, he has established the Placido Domingo World Competition in Vienna, which provides a great opportunity for those who have yet to achieve widespread exposure on the concert stage. He is far from threatened by the younger generation: "When you have been around in the business as long as I have, it is wonderful to know that there is so much talent in the next generation coming up behind you."

Yet his schedule as operatic performer is as full as ever, with more new challenges on the horizon. Indeed he maintains that he is learning more new operas now, at the age of 54, than at any time since the beginning of his career. With new performances of *Il Guarany* by Carlos Gomes, a Brazilian composer, Massenet's *Hérodiade*, Mozart's *Idomeneo*, and Verdi's *Simon Boccanegra* in the 1994–95 season, Domingo is obviously not ready to settle into the administrator's chair just yet. He also has plans for conducting *The Flying Dutchman* and singing in *Tristan und Isolde* in the near future. His unflagging commitment to opera and love of the stage have been the inspiration for this modern renaissance man's boundless energy and enthusiasm.

LEFT: *"Look Ma, I'm a star!" Domingo joined the pantheon of Hollywood greats as he received his star on the Hollywood Walk of Fame, September 2nd, 1993. Hollywood Chamber of Commerce official Bill Welch is at his right.*

ABOVE: *Domingo sings his heart out for the World Cup, summer 1994. His favorite team, of course, is Spain, a preference he shares with fellow Spaniard José Carreras.*

THE GREATEST TENORS

PREVIOUS PAGES: *The world's most famous tenors announce they will reunite after four years on the eve of the 1994 World Cup final.*

ABOVE: *Singing for a cause: The Elizabeth Taylor Aids Foundation was the beneficiary of all money raised from the tenors' concert in Los Angeles. The money is being used to build a new medical facility for AIDS sufferers in Los Angeles.*

RIGHT: *Pavarotti and Domingo share the stage for opening night at the Metropolitan Opera, September 27th, 1993. It was the 25th anniversary of both men's Met debuts and climaxed with a thrilling rendition of Act III of* Il Trovatore, *with the tenors alternating in the part of Manrico.*

July 7th, 1990 was a day to remember in the annals of opera history. "The world's three greatest tenors," as they have now been dubbed, Luciano Pavarotti, Placido Domingo, and José Carreras met at the Caracalla Baths in Rome, Italy for their first performance together. Operatic recitals do not usually make world news – but this one was special, not only because it marked the end of the 1990 World Cup, probably the world's most popular sporting event, but because in this world of large egos, sharing the limelight with artistic rivals was practically unheard of.

If you examine the lives and experiences of the tenors, some striking similarities appear. All were inspired at an early age to become performers: Pavarotti by Beniamino Gigli whose rehearsal he ecstatically witnessed; Carreras by Mario Lanza in the movie *The Great Caruso*; and Domingo by his parents, Spanish *zarzuela* singers. Carreras and Domingo, both Spaniards by birth, spent time at an early age in

Central America, both feel strongly about their heritage as Spaniards. The families from which the performers emerged were certainly not privileged, and all the performers worked in other professions on their way to the top.

In terms of their career paths, however, there are definite distinctions which can be made between the men. Domingo initially trained in Mexico and gained his first exposure in Israel, before performing widely across Europe. Carreras trained exclusively in Spain before moving on to the rest of Europe, where he felt most at home with Herbert von Karajan in Vienna. Pavarotti gained his first experience in Italy, and then quickly traveled to the English-speaking world, with debuts in England, Australia, and America.

Each of the men has chosen a well-defined repertoire as well. Pavarotti specializes in light Italian opera and operetta, and has been highly successful in operas such as *La Fille du Régiment* and *L'Elisir d'Amore*. These have pro-

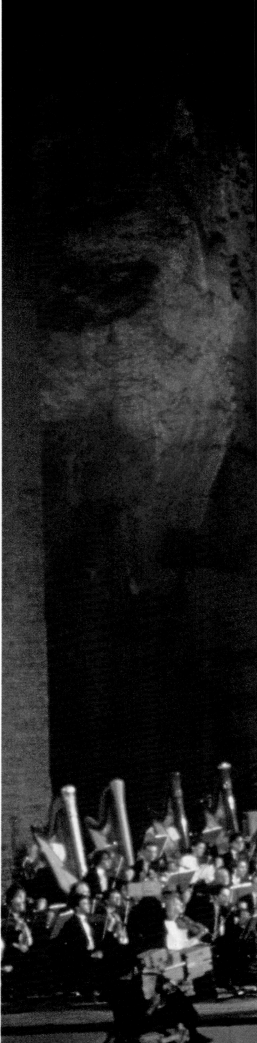

PREVIOUS PAGES: *The tenors applaud the orchestra, the combined forces of the Teatro del Opera di Roma and Maggio Musicale Fiorentino.*

ABOVE: *In September, 1991, Domingo and Pavarotti appeared together in a Metropolitan Opera House Gala concert. They excited audiences with the male voice duet from Act IV of Puccini's* La Bohème.

RIGHT: *The Baths of Caracalla made a wonderfully romantic backdrop to the historic collaboration between the tenors. The weather was clear and the night full of stars – what more could the promoters hope for?*

vided a showcase for his virtuosity, while making few demands on him as an actor. He has also tended to favor recital performances in the last few years, as opposed to operatic roles.

Domingo, on the other hand, has sung in over 80 different operatic roles, and tends to concentrate on the more tragic ones: Otello in *Otello* and Canio in *Pagliacci*, for example. He does some recital work, although these tend to be benefit or special gala performances. In recent years, he has made considerable time for other endeavors, such as conducting and artistic advisorship.

Carreras has been more of a generalist, although his greatest portrayals have been in the nineteenth-century French and Italian repertoire: *Carmen, La Bohème,* and *Un Ballo in Maschera.* He is a favorite on the recital as well as the operatic stage, although the greater

intimacy of the recital hall seems to suit him well.

Perhaps the most interesting similarity between the men is the way in which they have used and increased their fame so as to become "household names" instead of merely talented opera singers. Opera singers of the past, such as Mario Lanza and Ezio Pinza, have used popular mediums, such as movies and records, to increase their exposure to a mass audience. The dominance of huge entertainment conglomerates, such as Thorn EMI, Decca, and Sony, has changed the magnitude of this exposure, however. With their ability to distribute recordings and videos worldwide at short notice in massive quantities, and their enormous advertising and publicity budgets, they have the power to make a singer famous overnight.

Pavarotti, Domingo, and Carreras received their initial exposure through their operatic recordings, but are far better known among the public at large through their albums of popular songs. Pavarotti with Frank Sinatra, Domingo with John Denver, and Carreras with Kiri Te Kanawa in Leonard Bernstein's *West Side Story* and *South Pacific* are the performances that made the record companies and the performers more money than any operatic record, and helped to increase the popularity of

PAGES 62-63: *Domingo appears on a super-size TV screen as twilight falls on the night of the tenors' concert at Dodger Stadium, 1994.*

LEFT: *The battle of the high Cs rages as the tenors engage in a medley that sounded like a game of melodic table tennis at times.*

ABOVE: *This unique combination of artists had fans paying hundreds of dollars for tickets. The men have not indicated their plans for the 1998 World Cup, but a word to the wise: order your tickets now!*

FOLLOWING PAGES: *The colorful opening ceremony of the 1994 World Cup. The competition was held in the United States for first time in history.*

ABOVE: *As they rehearse during a sound check, the tenors look decidedly informal. Despite the southern Californian heat, Carreras and Pavarotti are careful to keep their throats warm.*

ABOVE, FAR RIGHT: *Dodger Stadium was the venue of choice for the concert. Its open back meant that sound was allowed to escape, avoiding unnecessary reverberations.*

FAR RIGHT: *The tenors announce in a New York press conference that they will reunite for their first concert in four years on the eve of the 1994 World Cup.*

opera in the 1980s. This popularity in turn spawned endorsements for American Express and Blackglama Furs by Pavarotti, and Rolex watches by Domingo. Carreras has not received this sort of exposure as much, perhaps because his career has been more concentrated in Europe.

All of the men have turned to television and film to widen their exposure. Pavarotti was among one of the first artists to tap into the mass media with his appearances on Johnny Carson's "The Tonight Show," "Live from Lincoln Center," "Sixty Minutes," and the movie *Yes, Giorgio.* Domingo appeared on a live television special celebrating another great tenor, Enrico Caruso, as well as at President Mitterand's inaug-

uration ceremony to sing the "Marseillaise." Carreras appeared in *The Final Romance,* a movie based on the life of tenor Julián Gayarre, as well as popular documentaries about the making of *West Side Story* and *South Pacific* with Leonard Bernstein. None of the men seem especially comfortable with these types of appearances, although they claim to enjoy them and audiences continue to tune in. Pavarotti seems to fare the best away from the rarefied atmosphere of the concert hall, perhaps because people can identify with "Pavarotti the peasant," a lover of wine, women, song, and spaghetti.

The rivalry between the men seems to have developed because the record company executives and concert pro-

ABOVE: *The rehearsal at the Baths of Caracalla, Rome, 1990. The medleys were the highpoint of the concert for many fans.*

ABOVE, FAR RIGHT: *With Zubin Mehta conducting, the tenors are in safe and capable hands.*

FAR RIGHT: *The tenors join in a medley together. This 1994 concert also featured the chorus of the Los Angeles Music Center Opera, an organization which has employed Domingo as its Artistic Consultant since 1984.*

moters need to label one of them "the world's greatest tenor." However, before their first concert together in Rome, which was seen by many as a "kiss-and-make-up" gesture, all of the men denied that they were in competition with the others. Of course they all said that the world can happily love and support more than one tenor, but there were incidents which indicated that they really thought otherwise. Domingo and Carreras disagreed about the order in which they were to appear for a gala concert in Vienna, a dispute which was not easily forgotten. When Kurt Herbert Adler, director of the San

Francisco Opera said that Pavarotti was the best tenor in the world, Domingo refused to appear there for a period. There was another incident at a performance by Domingo where Pavarotti's agents had taken out an advertisement, billing him as "the world's greatest tenor" in the concert program. Domingo refused to perform unless the advertisement was removed.

Most of these petty disagreements faded away when Carreras fell ill with leukemia in 1987. Both Domingo and Pavarotti by that point in their lives had experienced some brush with mortality which made them re-evaluate their

BELOW: *Domingo, Carreras, Mehta, and Pavarotti wave to the standing ovation that followed their 1994 performance. Pavarotti clasps his hands in his familiar gesture of thanks.*

priorities: Pavarotti was involved in a near-fatal plane crash in Milan in 1975 and Domingo had witnessed the death of many of his family members in the Mexican earthquake of 1985. The realization that Carreras was gravely ill brought the three men into contact — Pavarotti called often and Domingo even flew to visit him in Seattle. After Carreras recovered, he had the idea to

bring his colleagues together for a gala performance for the World Cup in 1990.

The promoters said that they would never get the three men to appear on the same stage. When Carreras told them about the prospect, however, they quickly agreed to appear and to donate their normal fees to charity. "We did it for the cup," said Pavarotti. All of the men are enormous soccer fans. Indeed

Carreras has described soccer as "not just a sport, but a social phenomena." Pavarotti is a supporter of the Italian team Juventus of Turin and goes to their matches whenever he can. He is an avid watcher of soccer on television as well, as his busy schedule keeps him away from the pitch most Saturdays. A weekly call to Italy on Sundays is part of his routine when he is out of the country, to

catch up on all the games and scores he has missed. Domingo, an ardent supporter of Spanish football, spent his 43rd birthday playing soccer with his sons and the great center-forward Hans Krankl in Vienna. He and Krankl made a deadly double act and Domingo demonstrated that if he had not devoted his life to opera, perhaps he could have been a soccer star.

The concert was to be held in the floodlit ruin of the Baths of Caracalla. This ancient site was perfect for the larger-than-life performance and provided ample room for the television crews. Maestro Zubin Mehta was chosen to conduct the combined Teatro del Opera di Roma and Maggio Musicale Fiorentino orchestras. He was asked to perform because of his natural